I0500541

TRUCKING THROUGH REGULATIONS

MASTERING DOT COMPLIANCE FOR A SAFER JOURNEY

2023
DOBBS MEDIA

Table of Contents

1. Introduction

The Department of Transportation (DOT) stands as a central pillar in ensuring the safe and efficient operation of various transportation systems within the United States. For trucking companies, adherence to DOT guidelines and regulations isn't merely an option; it's an obligation that carries significant weight, both for the safety of the general public and the longevity and reputation of the company.

Importance of DOT Compliance:

DOT compliance primarily ensures the safety and well-being of both the drivers and the general public. The guidelines set by the DOT are a culmination of years of research, analysis, and real-world observations. By adhering to these regulations, trucking companies:

- **Enhance Safety**: This is paramount. Given the size and potential danger associated with large commercial vehicles, ensuring they operate safely helps prevent accidents, injuries, and fatalities.

- **Promote Efficiency**: DOT regulations are designed not only with safety in mind but also the smooth flow of inter and intra-state commerce. Efficient transport routes, well-rested drivers, and well-maintained vehicles all contribute to more efficient delivery systems and reduced traffic congestion.

- **Protect Company Reputation**: Companies known for strict adherence to DOT regulations are viewed more favorably in the business world. They're considered reliable and trustworthy, leading to potentially more business opportunities.

- **Avoid Financial Liabilities**: Accidents, damages, and lawsuits can have a significant financial impact on a company. By being compliant, companies can reduce the risk of these financial burdens.

Consequences of Non-Compliance:

Choosing to ignore or not adequately adhere to DOT regulations can have dire consequences. These can range from financial penalties to more severe legal repercussions, all of which can jeopardize the continuity of a business. Consequences include:

- **Fines and Penalties**: The DOT can levy heavy fines on companies found to be non-compliant. These fines can range from hundreds to tens of thousands of dollars, depending on the severity of the violation.

- **Reduced Operational Authority**: In severe cases, a company's operational authority can be suspended or revoked, meaning they can no longer legally operate.

- **Increased Scrutiny**: Non-compliant companies may find themselves under increased observation, leading to more frequent inspections and audits.

- **Legal Repercussions**: In cases where non-compliance leads to severe accidents or fatalities, company stakeholders might face legal actions, potentially resulting in jail time.

- **Damaged Reputation**: In today's age of information, news of non-compliance can spread quickly, severely damaging a company's reputation and standing in the industry. This can lead to a loss of business partners, clients, and revenue.

In summary, DOT compliance is not just a bureaucratic requirement; it's a foundational aspect of any trucking company's operations, underpinning its commitment to safety, efficiency, and professionalism. Non-compliance, on the other hand, not only jeopardizes the company's standing but poses a real threat to public safety.

2. Registration and Licensing

The regulatory framework established by the Department of Transportation (DOT) mandates several registration and licensing requirements for trucking companies. These steps are designed to ensure that all entities operating commercial motor vehicles (CMVs) are held accountable to specific standards. Let's delve into the crucial aspects of this process:

Acquiring a USDOT Number:

A USDOT number is a unique identifier assigned to entities engaging in interstate, and in some cases, intrastate commerce. This number is especially vital for companies involved in the transportation of passengers or the hauling of cargo.

Procedures to Acquire a USDOT Number:

1. **Determine Eligibility**: Before applying, determine if your business requires a USDOT number. Generally, if your vehicle transports hazardous materials or exceeds a certain gross

vehicle weight rating and operates interstate, a USDOT number will be necessary.

2. **Online Registration**: Access the Federal Motor Carrier Safety Administration (FMCSA) online registration system. New users will need to set up an account.

3. **Complete the Application**: The online application (MCS-150) will request details about your company, the type of cargo you transport, and the scope of your operations.

4. **Submission & Review**: Once submitted, the FMCSA will review your application. Ensure that all provided information is accurate to avoid delays.

5. **Receive Your USDOT Number**: If approved, the number will be issued immediately through the online system. Ensure that this number is displayed correctly on all your commercial vehicles.

Motor Carrier (MC) Number Requirements:

Beyond the USDOT number, some carriers might also require an MC number, especially if they're transporting passengers for a fee or hauling regulated commodities across state lines.

Procedures to Obtain an MC Number:

1. **Determine Necessity**: Not every trucking company requires an MC number. It's mostly for those engaged in for-hire transportation, either of passengers or regulated freight.

2. **File an Application**: Access the FMCSA's Unified Registration System (URS) to complete the OP-1 Application for Motor Property Carrier and Broker Authority.

3. **Pay the Associated Fee**: There's a fee associated with obtaining an MC number. Ensure you make the necessary payment through the URS.

4. **Obtain Insurance**: For your MC number to become active, you must have the required insurance and bonding. The FMCSA will not

grant authority until they receive proof of this insurance.

5. **Wait for Approval**: After submitting all necessary documents and information, the FMCSA will take some time to review the application. Upon approval, you'll receive your MC number.

Intrastate vs. Interstate Operations:

- **Intrastate Operations**: Refers to commercial transportation that takes place solely within one state's boundaries. It does not cross state lines or involve any foreign country. Intrastate operators often have to abide by their state's specific regulatory requirements, which can vary significantly.

- **Interstate Operations**: This pertains to commercial transportation that crosses state lines or involves transport between the U.S. and another country. Companies involved in interstate operations need to comply with federal DOT regulations.

Procedures for Determining Operation Type:

1. **Evaluate Your Operations**: Regularly review routes and destinations to ascertain if your operations remain intrastate or if they've expanded to cross state boundaries.

2. **Compliance with Applicable Laws**: Once determined, ensure you comply with either state-specific regulations (for intrastate) or federal regulations (for interstate). This may involve acquiring permits, licenses, or undergoing specific inspections.

3. **Regular Review**: Regularly assess your operations, especially if you expand or change your service areas. This ensures you remain compliant at all times.

In essence, registration and licensing are foundational to the legal operation of a trucking business. Regularly reviewing and ensuring you possess the appropriate credentials not only keeps you in good standing with regulatory agencies but underscores a commitment to professionalism and legitimacy in the industry.

3. Driver Qualifications and Training

For a trucking company to maintain safety and uphold DOT compliance, stringent attention to driver qualifications and continuous training is vital. Comprehensive guidelines have been provided by the DOT and FMCSA to ensure trucking operations enlist competent, qualified, and well-trained drivers.

Driver's Age and Experience Requirements:

- **Minimum Age**: For interstate operations, a driver must be at least 21 years old. For intrastate operations, the minimum age may vary (typically 18), depending on state regulations.

- **Experience**: FMCSA does not explicitly outline a required duration of experience, but most trucking companies demand a specific duration of prior driving experience, depending on the type of vehicle and cargo.

Procedures for Age and Experience Verification:

1. **Document Collection**: Obtain and verify identification documents of prospective drivers for age validation.

2. **Driving History Examination**: Acquire a detailed driving history to ensure a consistent safe driving record.

3. **Reference Validation**: For experience confirmation, contact past employers and cross-check with the details provided by the potential hire.

Commercial Driver's License (CDL) Requirements:

- A CDL is mandatory for operating any CMV. CDLs are classified as Class A, Class B, and Class C, each specific to the type and weight of the vehicle, and the kind of cargo being transported.

Procedures for CDL Verification:

1. **CDL Document Procurement**: Obtain detailed CDL information during the hiring phase.

2. **Validity Confirmation**: Authenticate the CDL's validity and category through the respective state's DMV or the FMCSA's CDLIS.

3. **Regular Monitoring**: Keep track of CDL expiration dates and any necessary endorsements for unique cargoes, ensuring timely renewals.

Driver's Medical Examination and Certificate:

- A DOT-approved medical examiner must assess all drivers to ensure they are medically fit. If found fit, they are granted a Medical Examiner's Certificate (MEC).

Procedures for Medical Examination and MEC:

1. **Examination Scheduling**: Organize medical examinations for new and existing drivers, adhering to DOT intervals.

2. **MEC Collection and Storage**: Secure copies of the MEC, storing them systematically in the driver's personal file.

3. **Expiration Monitoring**: Diligently track the MEC's expiration dates, scheduling renewals in a timely manner.

Driver Training and Ongoing Education Programs:

- Initial training for novices and continuous educational initiatives for seasoned drivers are paramount for maintaining safety standards.

Procedures for Training and Continuous Education:

1. **Orientation and Training**: For new hires, facilitate a robust training program detailing vehicle operation, safety measures, and company protocols.

2. **Annual Refresher Programs**: Conduct regular sessions updating drivers on new regulations, safety practices, and other pertinent changes.

3. **Specialized Modules**: For specialized cargoes, such as hazardous materials, ensure drivers undergo niche training and acquire the necessary endorsements.

Driver Qualification File (DQF):

Every driver employed by the company must have an associated DQF as mandated by the FMCSA.

Essential Components of a DQF:

1. **Driver's Application for Employment**: This should be as detailed as possible, including previous employment details, CDL information, and any history of traffic violations or accidents.

2. **Inquiries to Previous Employers**: Written records of inquiries made to past employers about the driver's safety performance and drug/alcohol violations in the past three years.

3. **Driver's Road Test Certificate or Equivalent**: Documentation proving the driver successfully completed a road test for the CMV he/she will be operating.

4. **Motor Vehicle Record (MVR)**: An annual review of the driver's driving record to ensure they meet the company's safety standards.

5. **Medical Examiner's Certificate**: Proof that the driver is medically fit to operate a CMV.

6. **Drug and Alcohol Testing Records**: All results and documentation associated with drug and alcohol testing.

7. **Annual Driver Record Review**: A yearly written review of the driver's performance.

8. **Training Certificates and Endorsements**: Documentation of any specialized training sessions attended and all endorsements acquired.

Procedures for Maintaining and Storing DQFs:

1. **Organized Filing System**: Implement a systematic, secure storage method (digital/physical) to ensure easy retrieval of driver files.

2. **Regular Updates**: Promptly integrate any new documents, certificates, or training records into the existing DQF.

3. **Duration of Storage**: Abide by FMCSA guidelines regarding the retention duration of DQFs, even post-termination of a driver's employment.

By meticulously adhering to these procedures and maintaining a comprehensive DQF for every driver, trucking companies can promote safety, professionalism, and, importantly, stay compliant with all regulatory standards.

4. Vehicle Maintenance and Inspection

Maintaining and inspecting vehicles are not just prerequisites for DOT compliance but are foundational for ensuring the safety of drivers, cargo, and the general public. Proper vehicle upkeep reduces breakdowns, enhances efficiency, and minimizes costly repairs. Here's a comprehensive look at the essential aspects of vehicle maintenance and inspection.

Regular Maintenance Schedule:

Every vehicle has a unique maintenance schedule, often recommended by the manufacturer, which covers everything from oil changes to more intricate system checks.

Procedures:

1. **Develop a Calendar**: Based on the manufacturer's recommendations and vehicle usage, set up a maintenance calendar. This will ensure that no essential check-ups are missed.

2. **Regular Check-ups**: At least once a month, conduct basic check-ups including fluid levels, brake systems, tires, and lights.

3. **Professional Service**: Depending on the vehicle's usage, schedule professional servicing quarterly or bi-annually.

Suggestions for File Retention:

- **Digital Tracking**: Implement fleet management software that automatically tracks and reminds of upcoming maintenance.

- **Physical Records**: Keep a maintenance logbook in each vehicle, ensuring drivers or maintenance personnel record every service or repair.

Pre-trip and Post-trip Inspection Requirements:

The FMCSA mandates these inspections to ensure that vehicles are roadworthy before and after each trip.

Procedures:

1. **Checklist Development**: Create a comprehensive checklist for drivers detailing essential inspection points like brakes, tires,

lights, mirrors, and any cargo-related equipment.

2. **Driver Training**: Train drivers on how to thoroughly conduct both pre-trip and post-trip inspections.

3. **Reporting**: Any issues or potential problems identified during these inspections should be reported immediately.

Suggestions for File Retention:

- **Inspection Logs**: Maintain daily logs of both pre-trip and post-trip inspections.

- **Issue Reports**: Any issues reported should have an associated documentation detailing the problem and subsequent repairs.

Annual Vehicle Inspections:

A more rigorous, detailed examination of the vehicle, often by an external agency or a certified professional, is mandated annually.

Procedures:

1. **Schedule Inspections**: Based on the purchase date or the last inspection date, set a yearly reminder for the inspection.

2. **Certified Inspectors**: Only utilize FMCSA-approved inspectors or entities for these inspections.

3. **Address Issues Promptly**: Any issues unearthed during this inspection should be rectified immediately.

Suggestions for File Retention:

- **Certification Storage**: Store the inspection certification in both the vehicle and in a centralized office location.

- **Digital Back-up**: Scan and save digital copies of all certifications, especially if the fleet size is considerable.

Record Keeping for All Vehicle Maintenance:

Meticulous record-keeping isn't just a regulatory mandate; it can be invaluable for tracking vehicle performance, predicting potential issues, and making informed decisions about vehicle replacement or major repairs.

Procedures:

1. **Centralized Repository**: Create a single, organized location (physical or digital) where all vehicle maintenance records are stored.

2. **Regular Updates**: Every service, repair, inspection, or maintenance activity should be immediately documented and stored.

3. **Annual Reviews**: Conduct an annual review of each vehicle's maintenance records to assess vehicle health and performance.

Suggestions for File Retention:

- **Cloud Storage**: Utilize cloud storage solutions for digital records, ensuring data redundancy and easy access.

- **Physical Archive**: If maintaining physical records, utilize labeled binders for each vehicle, stored in a moisture-free, organized environment.

- **Retention Duration**: As per FMCSA regulations, retain maintenance and inspection records for a minimum of one year for the vehicle's active service and six months after the vehicle leaves the service.

In essence, a diligent approach to vehicle maintenance and inspection not only ensures DOT compliance but actively prolongs vehicle life, guarantees safety, and optimizes operational efficiency.

5. Hours of Service Regulations

The Hours of Service (HOS) regulations, established by the FMCSA, exist to combat driver fatigue, a significant contributor to accidents in the trucking realm. Ensuring a thorough understanding and adherence to these rules is essential for maintaining the safety of drivers and the wider public.

Maximum Driving Hours:

For property-carrying drivers:

- **11-hour driving limit**: After 10 consecutive hours off duty, drivers are permitted a maximum of 11 hours of drive time.

- **14-hour window**: From the onset of their workday, drivers have a 14-hour window in which they can drive. Post this window, driving is not allowed, even if they haven't maxed out the 11-hour drive limit.

Procedures:

1. **Driver Scheduling**: When mapping routes, ensure no driver is scheduled to drive over the 11-hour limit within a 14-hour window.

2. **Consistent Monitoring**: Regularly cross-check ELD records or logbooks to validate compliance with this stipulation.

Break and Rest Period Mandates:

- **30-minute break rule**: Property-carrying drivers who accumulate 8 hours of driving time without a break of at least 30 minutes are required to rest before resuming.

- **34-hour restart**: A 34+ consecutive hour off-duty period allows drivers to reset a 7/8 consecutive day period.

Procedures:

1. **Break Notifications**: If utilizing ELDs, set them to notify drivers as they approach the 8-hour driving mark without a break.

2. **Integrate Breaks into Schedules**: Design trip plans with designated breaks, ensuring

alignment with regulations and avoiding unplanned halts.

Sleeper Berth Provisions:

- **Off-duty time split**: Drivers can divide their 10-hour off-duty time. One stretch must be at least 2 hours, and the other a consecutive 7 hours in the sleeper berth. Cumulatively, the two should amount to 10 hours minimum.

Procedures:

1. **Inform Drivers**: Offer comprehensive training to drivers about the sleeper berth provision and the correct way to document their time.

2. **Ensure Vehicle Suitability**: For operators taking advantage of the sleeper berth provision, vehicles should come fitted with appropriate sleeper facilities.

Electronic Logging Devices (ELD) Requirements:

- **Mandatory Implementation**: ELDs are essential for drivers obligated to maintain Records of Duty Status (RODS), which is a detailed log of a driver's working hours, ensuring drivers don't exceed the legal limit set by FMCSA.

- **Data Documentation**: ELDs autonomously capture driving hours, providing precise HOS tracking.

Procedures for ELD Implementation:

1. **Set Up ELDs**: Install FMCSA-endorsed ELDs in all vehicles necessitating RODS.

2. **Orient Drivers**: Instruct drivers on ELD operation, including logging diverse statuses, potential edits, and certification processes.

3. **Regular Data Examination**: Periodically assess and backup ELD data, ensuring alignment with regulations and timely identification of any infringements.

ELD Usage Mandates and Exemptions:

- **Necessity**: ELDs are crucial for most drivers obligated to maintain RODS.

- **Exemptions**: Drivers utilizing paper RODS for no more than 8 days within any 30-day period, operators of vehicles manufactured prior to

2000, those engaged in drive-away-tow-away functions, and some short-haul drivers.

Popular ELD Providers

1. **KeepTruckin**
2. **Samsara**
3. **Geotab**
4. **Teletrac Navman**
5. **Omnitracs**
6. **J.J. Keller**

By meticulously observing the Hours of Service regulations and tapping into the sophisticated functions of contemporary ELD systems, trucking enterprises can foster road safety, prioritize driver well-being, and ensure unwavering compliance with FMCSA directives.

6. Drug and Alcohol Testing

The FMCSA has stringent guidelines regarding drug and alcohol testing to ensure safety on the roads. Ensuring that drivers are not under the influence is not only a matter of compliance but also a moral responsibility for the safety of the general public and the driver themselves.

Required Drug and Alcohol Testing Processes:

All drivers who operate commercial motor vehicles (CMVs) are subject to drug and alcohol testing to detect the use of illegal drugs and misuse of alcohol.

Procedures:

1. **Selecting Testing Facilities**: Choose only certified laboratories and testing facilities to ensure accuracy and reliability.

2. **Informing Drivers**: Clearly communicate the drug and alcohol testing requirements and policies to all drivers.

3. **Maintaining Confidentiality**: Ensure that all test results are kept confidential and are disclosed only to authorized personnel.

Pre-employment, Random, Post-accident, and Reasonable Suspicion Testing:

- **Pre-employment**: Before hiring, potential drivers must undergo drug testing. They can only be employed upon receiving a negative result.

- **Random Testing**: Drivers must be randomly tested throughout the year. The selection process should be unannounced and spread evenly throughout the year.

- **Post-accident**: Drivers are tested following accidents to determine if drugs or alcohol played a role.

- **Reasonable Suspicion**: If a trained supervisor or company official believes a driver is under the influence, the driver can be tested.

Procedures:

1. **Establish Testing Criteria**: Create clear criteria for each testing type and ensure that

supervisors are trained in identifying signs of drug or alcohol impairment.

2. **Documentation**: Keep thorough records of each testing event, from the reason for the test to its result.

3. **Prompt Action**: If a driver tests positive, remove them from safety-sensitive functions immediately until they complete the return-to-duty process.

Return-to-duty Process:

A driver who has violated the prohibited drug and alcohol standards must complete the return-to-duty process, which includes evaluation, treatment, return-to-duty testing, and follow-up tests.

Procedures:

1. **Immediate Removal**: Drivers who violate standards should be removed from duty immediately.

2. **SAP Consultation**: Direct the driver to a Substance Abuse Professional (SAP) for assessment and recommendations.

3. **Complete Recommended Treatment**: Ensure that the driver completes the recommended treatment or counseling.

4. **Return-to-duty Testing**: Before returning to duty, the driver must have a negative result in the return-to-duty drug or alcohol test.

5. **Follow-up Testing**: Conduct at least six unannounced tests in the first 12 months following the driver's return to duty.

Substance Abuse Professional (SAP) Roles:

SAPs play a crucial role in ensuring drivers are fit to return to work after a drug or alcohol violation. They evaluate the driver, recommend treatment, and provide a follow-up evaluation.

Procedures:

1. **Choosing a SAP**: Ensure that the SAP is qualified and credentialed as per the FMCSA guidelines.

2. **Maintain Open Communication**: Keep open lines of communication between the SAP and the company to monitor the driver's progress.

3. **Documentation**: Record all interactions and evaluations associated with the SAP.

File Retention:

All records of drug and alcohol testing should be stored securely to maintain confidentiality and for future reference.

Procedures for File Retention:

1. **Storage System**: Establish a secure digital or physical filing system where all test results, evaluations, and other pertinent information are stored.

2. **Duration**: As per FMCSA regulations:

   - Negative test results: Retain for a minimum of one year.

   - Positive test results: Retain for a minimum of five years.

3. **Access Control**: Limit access to these files, ensuring only authorized personnel can view them.

By meticulously observing the FMCSA's drug and alcohol testing regulations, trucking companies not only ensure compliance but also foster a safe and healthy work environment for their drivers and safer roads for all.

7. Safety and Operational Policies

Safety is a paramount concern in the trucking industry. Ensuring drivers and the public are protected through comprehensive policies and training is an ethical obligation and a regulatory requirement.

Safety Training Programs for Drivers:

Driver training is the backbone of any safety-first trucking operation. A well-trained driver is less likely to commit violations and more likely to operate their vehicle safely and efficiently.

Procedures:

1. **Onboarding Training**: Every new driver should undergo an intensive safety training program when they join the company. This should include both classroom and practical on-road training.

2. **Refresher Courses**: Annually, or as needed, drivers should attend refresher courses to stay updated on the latest safety standards and practices.

3. **Specialized Training**: Offer specialized training modules for different scenarios, such as driving in hazardous conditions, handling specific cargo types, or operating specialized equipment.

4. **Monitoring & Feedback**: Use telematics and feedback from supervisors to identify areas where individual drivers may need additional training.

Equipment Safety Requirements:

The condition of a truck or any equipment can directly influence safety. Ensuring they are up to safety standards is crucial.

Procedures:

1. **Regular Inspections**: Have a routine in place for daily or weekly inspections of all equipment.

2. **Maintenance Schedules**: Based on the manufacturer's recommendations and usage, set up regular maintenance schedules for all equipment.

3. **Immediate Repairs**: Address and repair any safety concerns or malfunctions immediately.

Avoid allowing any compromised equipment to be in use.

4. **Safety Kits**: Equip each truck with essential safety kits, including fire extinguishers, reflective triangles, and first-aid kits.

Load Securement Standards:

Improperly secured loads can pose significant risks. Adhering to the FMCSA's regulations on cargo securement is essential.

Procedures:

1. **Training**: Educate drivers on the correct techniques and equipment for securing different types of loads.

2. **Regular Checks**: Drivers should inspect cargo securement at the beginning of a trip, after the first 50 miles, after breaks, and every three hours or 150 miles thereafter.

3. **Use of Equipment**: Use tie-downs, blocking, bracing, and other securement methods as per the nature of the cargo.

4. **Documentation**: Maintain a checklist for load securement that drivers can fill out, ensuring that all measures have been taken.

Emergency Response Protocols:

In the event of emergencies, having a set protocol can make the difference between a contained situation and a major catastrophe.

Procedures:

1. **Emergency Training**: Conduct regular emergency response drills for drivers, simulating scenarios like accidents, fires, or hazardous material leaks.

2. **Emergency Contacts**: Equip each truck with a list of emergency contacts, including local authorities, the company's central office, and medical facilities.

3. **Incident Reporting**: Create a standardized incident report form that drivers can fill out after any emergency. This can help in understanding what went wrong and how to prevent it in the future.

4. **Post-Incident Review**: After any major incident, conduct a review with all stakeholders to identify areas for improvement in the response protocol.

By instilling rigorous safety and operational policies and ensuring adherence through regular monitoring and training, trucking companies can significantly reduce risks and uphold the highest standards of safety and efficiency in their operations.

8. Record Keeping

Effective record-keeping is not only a DOT compliance requirement but also an essential practice for any organized and efficient trucking company. It facilitates smooth operations, ensures that critical data is accessible when needed, and helps in protecting the company from potential liabilities. Here's a detailed look at several crucial record-keeping areas and the procedures for managing them.

Maintaining Driver Qualification Files (DQFs):

A DQF is a comprehensive collection of a driver's professional documents and credentials, which confirms their eligibility to operate commercial motor vehicles.

Procedures:

1. **Centralized Storage System**: Implement a centralized storage system, either digital or physical, where all DQFs are consistently stored.

2. **Regular Updates**: Schedule periodic checks, at least annually, to ensure all documents in the

DQF are current. Update any expired licenses, medical certificates, or other time-sensitive documents.

3. **Secure Storage**: Ensure that DQFs are kept in a secure location, with access restricted to authorized personnel only, to maintain confidentiality.

4. **Backup**: Regularly back up digital files and consider maintaining duplicates of physical files in a separate location.

Retaining Hours-of-Service Logs:

Hours-of-service logs are critical in ensuring drivers are not overworked, which can lead to fatigue-related accidents.

Procedures:

1. **Electronic Logging Devices (ELD)**: If not already in place, adopt ELDs, which automatically record driving hours and ensure accuracy and compliance.

2. **Regular Audits**: Conduct monthly audits of the logs to identify any potential violations or discrepancies.

3. **Retention Period**: Retain the logs for a minimum of six months, as required by DOT regulations.

4. **Secure and Easy Access**: Store the logs securely but ensure they can be accessed quickly, especially during DOT inspections.

Keeping Maintenance and Inspection Reports:

Maintaining a thorough record of all vehicle maintenance and inspections helps ensure the fleet's safety and can be invaluable during audits or inspections.

Procedures:

1. **Standardized Forms**: Use standardized forms or software for all maintenance and Inspection activities to ensure consistency.

2. **Scheduled Maintenance Logs**: Record every scheduled maintenance activity, noting down any parts replaced or repairs done.

3. **DVIR (Driver Vehicle Inspection Report)**: After each trip, store the DVIR and address any flagged issues promptly.

4. **Retention Period**: Keep these reports for a minimum of 12 months for active vehicles and for 6 months after a vehicle leaves service.

Storing Drug and Alcohol Testing Results:

These records are sensitive and must be handled with utmost confidentiality.

Procedures:

1. **Secure Storage**: Given the sensitive nature of these records, they should be stored in a highly secure location, separate from other files like the DQFs.

2. **Digital Encryption**: If stored electronically, ensure the files are encrypted and protected against unauthorized access.

3. **Access Control**: Limit access to these files to designated personnel who handle drug and alcohol program management.

4. **Retention Period**: Follow DOT guidelines on retention, which vary based on the type of test (e.g., negative test results are kept for a minimum of one year, while positive results are retained for five years).

In summary, meticulous record-keeping is both a legal requirement and a best practice for trucking companies. It ensures smooth operations, helps during audits and inspections, and can provide protection in legal scenarios.

9. Transportation of Hazardous Materials

The transportation of hazardous materials (HazMat) is a specialized area in the trucking industry, requiring heightened vigilance and adherence to specific regulations set forth by the DOT. Ensuring safety is paramount, given the potential risks these materials pose to the public, the environment, and the handlers themselves.

Special Training for HazMat Drivers:

Drivers transporting hazardous materials must have specialized training to understand the unique risks and requirements associated with their cargo.

Procedures:

1. **Mandatory HazMat Endorsement**: Ensure that all HazMat drivers possess a HazMat endorsement on their CDL (Commercial Driver's License).

2. **Initial Training**: Provide comprehensive training for drivers before they handle hazardous

materials. This should cover the nature of the materials, emergency procedures, and safe handling practices.

3. **Refresher Courses**: Schedule regular refresher training sessions, at least once every three years, to keep drivers updated on regulations and safety protocols.

4. **Training Documentation**: Keep records of all training sessions, including dates, content covered, and attendees. Retain these for a minimum of three years.

Packaging and Labeling Requirements:

Proper packaging and labeling are critical to ensure the safety of hazardous materials during transport.

Procedures:

1. **Use DOT-Approved Packaging**: Ensure that all hazardous materials are packaged in containers that meet DOT specifications and standards.

2. **Correct Labeling**: Clearly label each package with the necessary hazard class, identification number, and proper shipping name.

3. **Regular Inspection**: Before transport, inspect all packages for damage or leaks. Address any issues immediately and repack if necessary.

4. **Documentation**: Maintain a log of all materials packaged and labeled, noting down any discrepancies or issues addressed.

Shipping Papers and Documentation:

Accurate documentation ensures that everyone in the supply chain understands the nature and risks of the transported materials.

Procedures:

1. **Detailed Descriptions**: Ensure shipping papers provide a detailed description of the hazardous material, including its hazard class, UN/NA identification number, and quantity.

2. **Emergency Response Information**: Include emergency response information on the shipping papers, providing guidance on handling spills, exposures, or other incidents.

3. **Accessibility**: Drivers should keep shipping papers in a designated pouch or location in the

cab, ensuring they are easily accessible in case of inspection or emergency.

4. **Retention**: Retain copies of all shipping papers for at least 375 days after the material is shipped.

Placarding and Marking of Vehicles:

Correct placarding and marking provide immediate, visual information about the hazards associated with the transported material.

Procedures:

1. **Correct Placards**: Display the appropriate placards on all sides of the vehicle based on the hazard class of the transported material.

2. **Visibility and Condition**: Ensure placards are clean, legible, and free from damage. Replace faded or damaged placards immediately.

3. **Consistency**: Ensure that the markings and placards are consistent with the information on the shipping papers.

4. **Marking Storage**: Keep a set of various placards and markings readily available in the vehicle,

allowing drivers to switch them out based on the materials they're transporting.

In conclusion, transporting hazardous materials is a high-responsibility task, demanding specialized knowledge and meticulous adherence to safety protocols. Proper training, packaging, documentation, and placarding are essential in mitigating risks and ensuring safe transportation.

10. Conclusion and Ongoing Compliance

Ensuring DOT compliance isn't a one-time endeavor; it's a continual process that requires consistent attention, adaptation, and refinement. As the trucking landscape evolves, regulations shift, and business scales, companies must remain agile in their commitment to safety and regulatory adherence.

The Importance of Periodic Internal Audits:

Regular internal audits can spotlight areas of concern before they become critical issues or result in regulatory violations.

Procedures:

1. **Schedule Regular Audits**: Determine a schedule (e.g., annually, semi-annually) for comprehensive internal reviews of all compliance areas.

2. **Train Audit Teams**: Equip your internal teams with the necessary training and resources to effectively evaluate compliance levels.

3. **Action on Findings**: After each audit, promptly address any identified areas of concern or non-compliance. Set up a clear action plan and designate responsible teams or individuals.

4. **Documentation**: Maintain detailed records of all audits, findings, and corrective actions taken. This can be invaluable during external inspections or in benchmarking compliance progress.

Keeping Abreast of Regulatory Changes:

The regulatory landscape is dynamic, with changes, updates, and new additions occurring regularly.

Procedures:

1. **Subscription Services**: Subscribe to DOT newsletters or update services that notify subscribers about regulatory changes.

2. **Regular Training**: Incorporate any new regulations into your ongoing training programs, ensuring your staff stays updated.

3. **Engage in Industry Groups**: Participate in trucking industry groups or forums, which can

be valuable sources of information and best practices.

Seeking External Consultants or Compliance Services for Assistance:

External expertise can provide an objective view of your operations, highlighting potential blind spots.

Procedures:

1. **Identify Reputable Consultants**: Research and shortlist consultants or services with a proven track record in DOT compliance within the trucking industry.

2. **Regular Reviews**: Consider bringing in external experts for periodic reviews, separate from your internal audits, to gain a fresh perspective.

3. **Stay Open to Feedback**: External reviews can be eye-opening. Be receptive to feedback, even if it's critical, and use it as a tool for improvement.

Useful URLs:

1. **Federal Motor Carrier Safety Administration (FMCSA)**: https://www.fmcsa.dot.gov/

2. **Department of Transportation (DOT)**: https://www.transportation.gov/

3. **Pipeline and Hazardous Materials Safety Administration (PHMSA)**: https://www.phmsa.dot.gov/

4. **DOT's Office of Drug & Alcohol Policy & Compliance**: https://www.transportation.gov/odapc

5. **National Association of Small Trucking Companies (NASTC)**: https://www.nastc.com/

6. **Transportation Intermediaries Association (TIA)**: https://www.tianet.org/

In closing, DOT compliance is an ongoing journey that requires vigilance, adaptability, and a proactive approach. Leveraging both internal efforts and external expertise, while staying informed about regulatory shifts, ensures not only compliance but also promotes the safe, efficient operation of a trucking company.

www.ingramcontent.com/pod-product-compliance
Lightning Source LLC
Chambersburg PA
CBHW050518290526
45786CB00007B/2619